Songs of Grace and Redemption

John Donnelly's plays include *Bone* (Royal Court Theatre Upstairs), *Myrna Molloy* (Operating Theatre Company), *Showtime* (LAMDA) and *Heat and Light* (Heat and Light Company, Hampstead Theatre). He is a past winner of both the PMA Award for Best Writer and the NSDF *Sunday Times* Playwriting Award, and has recently completed an attachment at the National Theatre.

also by John Donnelly

BONE

JOHN DONNELLY

Songs of Grace and Redemption

in collaboration with
Liminal Theatre

faber and faber

First published in 2007
by Faber and Faber Limited
3 Queen Square, London WC1N 3AU

Typeset by Country Setting, Kingsdown, Kent CT14 8ES
Printed in England by Antony Rowe Limited

A CIP record for this book
is available from the British Library

ISBN 978-0-571-24093-7

2 4 6 8 10 9 7 5 3 1

Songs of Grace and Redemption, presented by Liminal Theatre, Time Won't Wait and Theatre 503, was first performed at Theatre 503, London, on 30 October 2007. The cast was as follows:

Peter Robert Reina
John Mark Springer
Nicola Natasha Alderslade
Steve James Hurn
Soley Hannah Young

All other parts played by members of the company

Directed by Janette Smith
Designed by Naomi Dawson
Lighting by Anna Watson
Music and Sound Design by Neil Codling
Producer Sarah Sansom

GRACE

Simple elegance or refinement of movement
Courteous goodwill
Free and unmerited favour (often of God)

Also, '*grace* period' – a period officially allowed
for payment of a sum due or for compliance
with a law or condition

REDEMPTION

The action of regaining or gaining possession of
something in exchange for payment or clearing a debt
The action of buying one's freedom

Characters

Peter
thirties

John
thirties

Nicola
thirty

Steve
thirties

Soley
twenties

Sarah, Claire, Chris, Dan,
Ailsa, Ralf, Barman, Rachel, Waitress

*The play is written for a cast of five.
The composition of the cast should reflect
the composition of the city.*

*It should be cast for the characters in bold above,
who then share the remaining parts. Sarah and Waitress
should be played by the same actress who plays Nicola.*

*The play is set in London, Birmingham, and
a part of Iceland so remote it does not have a name.*

*Set, props and costume should be minimal and
evocative to aid quick changes between scenes.*

SONGS OF GRACE AND REDEMPTION

For Cat

When what used to excite you does not
Like you've used up all your allowance
of experiences

Mark E. Smith,
'Just Step S'ways'

Part One

ONE

John and Nicola's kitchen. Evening.
  She wears a deliberately sexy dress and drinks from a bottle of cider. John is dressed smart-casual from work. He has a glass of wine.

Nicola I was at an awards ceremony. For the Business Woman of the Year Award. In this big . . . banqueting hall, in a hotel or something.

John An awards ceremony?

Nicola Yes.

John Like the Oscars.

Nicola And I won.

John Well done.

Nicola I was wearing a gown. And I looked beautiful, if you can imagine that. (*Beat.*) And there / were all these men.

John (Yeah, of course I can.)

Nicola All these men were staring at me. Thousands of them.

John Thousands?

Nicola I don't know – I'm not good with numbers, something like that.

John Was I there?

Nicola (*beat*) Yeah.

3

John You don't sound sure.

Nicola And all these men wanted to have me. But I chose you.
 I was telling you something.

John I thought you'd finished.

Nicola Are you annoyed with me?

John No.

Nicola You've hardly touched your three ninety-seven wine.

John I told you, it was half price, it's worth six ninety-eight.
 Enjoying your cider?

Nicola Is this about the conference?

John No.

Nicola If it means that much to you, bloody go to Birmingham.

John I think you should have your mind on tomorrow, that's all.

Nicola Can we not talk about tomorrow on a date night?

John Well, I think it's important.

Nicola You didn't even –

John I came from work.

Nicola You said you'd be home at six.

John I had stuff to finish. People depend on me, it's not advertising.

Nicola People depend on me.

John What? What are you looking at me like that for?

TWO

Soley's Bar.

Morning. Soley wears an alarming combination of girly pink, old school death or speed-metal T-shirts – tattoos and maybe piercings. She conducts a heated telephone argument, in Icelandic, on the bar phone – the kind one can have only with a lover or former lover. Her telephone dialogue should be considered as music, acting as a counterpoint to the scene. More dialogue (in Icelandic) may be incorporated at the discretion of the production.

Peter sits by the window. He sports garish lycra running gear and a rucksack. There are three shot glasses lined up before him, containing a clear liquid. He has a laptop. He builds a house of cards throughout.

Steve sits nearby, a case on the surface before him, next to an empty cup and saucer. He watches Soley.

Peter Germany.
Switzerland.
Italy.
Austria.
Czech Republic.
Poland.
Lithuania . . . Lithu–
Yeah, then Germany again, though not to stay obviously, then Denmark, hop, skip and a jump to Sweden (Malmo, up to Helsingborg).
Norway, Finland.

Gestures at Soley.

Iceland.

Drinks a shot, stares at Steve, who watches Soley.

Kiki Pinch.
Kiki Pinch, it's my stripper name, what's yours?

Nicola enters in a hurry. She looks for someone to serve her.

You on Facebook?

Steve No.

Soley *Hann er bjáni.* [He's full of shit.]

Peter You know there's free WiFi? It's actually the Catholics next door, but they've got no password. The immaculate connection I call it. S'pose they need one for all the kiddie porn.

Steve You think that's funny?

Nicola Hi –

Soley *Mjög fyndin.* [Very funny.]

Peter What's your name, I can poke you?
You can be my lesbian vampire mistress if you want.

Steve I told you I –

Peter I know.

Points as if to say, 'I know what you're thinking.'

'Who is this maverick?'

Nicola Excuse me –

Soley *Ég er pakklát.* [I'm grateful.]

Peter That's funny, when I did that you looked at my finger. Dogs do that. If you point, humans follow the line, but dogs just stare at the finger. Or lick it –

Steve I'm not licking your finger.

Peter I'm not asking you to lick my finger. Did I tell you I'm walking to every country on –

Steve Yes.

Nicola Excuse –

6

Soley *Bíddu.* [Wait.] I'm on the phone.

Nicola And I'm late for work.

Soley So get up earlier. (*Back into phone.*) *Éttu skít hálfviti, ég lagði mig í hættu fyrir þig.* [Eat shit, halfwit, I risked my neck for you.]

Peter My card.

Peter hands Steve his business card.

Steve 'Peter Trout. Wanderer.'

Peter But you can call me Kiki.

Soley *Nei, nei, nei.* [No, no, no.]
   Hvað sagðirðu? [What was that?] Motherfucker!

Soley ends argument abruptly, slamming phone down.

Nicola Look, I can see you're having as bad a day as I am, / but I would like a –

Soley storms past out back.

Oh, for –

Steve's phone rings. It has a silly ringtone. He answers.

Steve Sorry, the line's –

Peter I can channel the energy of the cosmos through my hands.

Steve No, it's your end, I've / got four bars.

The bar phone rings.

Peter It won't be this end, signal's like glass.

Steve Say again.

Peter It's bloody internet Stonehenge here.

Steve Can you shut up? No, not you. Hello.

Following quickly:

Nicola (*calling out to Soley, off*) Hello.

Steve Hello.

Nicola Hello.

Steve Hello.

Nicola Fuck's sake.

Nicola leaves. Steve redials.

Peter (*points at laptop*) See this. Triangulates my position by satellite. To the millimetre. So right now we are in . . . Iceland? Hang on, that's not . . .

Peter shakes the GPS. Steve gets voicemail, angrily.

Doesn't matter. (*Taps his heart.*) This is the only compass I need. Take my hand. Commune. I want you to feel my heart.

Steve What you doing?

Peter I have healing hands.

Steve What?

Peter I went to a Reiki class, they told me I had the gift.

Steve I don't like being touched, all right?

Peter You keep fingering it.

Steve What?

Peter The case. What's in it? Smack?

Steve You ask a lot of questions.

Peter I have a curious nature.

Steve answers his phone.

Steve Yeah, well, it ain't me, I got four bars. I said it's not me, I come here cause the signal's *ah shit*!

Steve texts. Soley enters, answers the phone, ends the call. Resets the phone. She polishes the counter furiously, humming.

Peter See my finger. Used to be a band there. That was my pain. Not any more. I took it away. You're in pain too, aren't you? You have a very negative energy, I can sense it.

Steve (*trying to attract Soley's attention*) Excuse me, how much is –

Soley brings Steve the bill, slams it down. Soley's mobile rings.

Thanks.

Peter Another couple of shots, please.

Soley Little early, isn't it?

Peter It's party time in Reykjavik.

Soley answers her phone.

Soley Reykjavik's an hour behind. (*Screams into phone.*) *Fábjáni!* [Idiot!] (*Hangs up.*) Besides, this is London.

Soley returns to the counter, pours herself a shot. Necks it. Slams it down.

Peter Isn't it just?

Soley pours herself another shot. Steve's phone vibrates. He checks the message. He leaves change on the saucer, prepares to leave. He texts again. Realises Peter is staring at him.

Steve Don't you have somewhere to go, a job or –

Peter Told you, I sold up and set off.

Steve (*texting*) Oh yeah, why's that?

Soley drinks.

Peter I found my dad shagging my missus.

Soley spits out her shot. Steve stops texting.

Sometimes at night, I'd leave them chatting and go off to bed. Come down later for a glass of water, find them doing spoons on the sofa. I thought it was dad being familial.

Soley brings the shots and the bill, and collects the empties. She catches Steve's eye.

Soley Sorry.

Steve 'S okay.

Peter So one day, come home from work, go upstairs, there they are. Like something from a porno.

Soley pretends not to hear this. Returns to the bar. Steve watches her. She watches Steve and Peter discreetly.

'Cept I'm an architect not a plumber.

Steve Yeah, and you haven't got a 'tache, neither.

Peter Four-pack of Guinness in one hand, bottle of Pinot Grigio in the other. 'Surprise!' Fuck me, was it. Two people I loved most in the world, staring straight at me.

Steve sends his text.

Steve How come they were both staring at you if they were –
Oh!

Peter Yeah. 'Oh.' And there was me worried Dad was lonely. Mum had died and, well –

Steve Still see him?

Peter Only when I close my eyes. Imagine. Your own father.

Steve What about your missus?

Peter No idea. Walked out the bedroom, didn't look back. I mean it, I left and . . . week later sold my half of the business. To Dad. We were partners. Maybe I'll go and see her.

Steve's phone vibrates. He checks another text.

Steve Your wife?

Peter No, my chiropractor.

Steve Got a bad back?

Peter This fabric's made from a semi-permeable membrane that maintains optimum body temperature while wicking the sweat away from the skin, keeping me dry and alleviating chafe. It's designed for extreme conditions. I used to build libraries. Now I'm building a monument to self-preservation. The new me. The new Peter Trout. I'm not dicking about. I'm walking to every country on earth.

Steve So what's stopping you?

Soley bangs down the shot glass on the table. The house of cards collapses.
Soley walks off. Steve watches her. Peter observes this. Steve notices Peter watching him.

Peter I could ask you the same question.

Steve What's stopping me doing what?

Peter Anything.

THREE

Forecourt. Steve's car, parked under a street lamp.
  Steve in the driver's seat, Sarah in the passenger seat.
He stares at her.

Steve . . . kids.

Sarah Steve. Can't say you want kids!

  Steve picks up a block of wood. He carves.

I'm the monger, not you.

Steve Don't say that word.

Sarah What, monger?

Steve Shouldn't say that.

Sarah You're carving. You're thinking about –

Steve I've got to go.

Sarah You still dream.

Steve What?

Sarah I hear you. At night. Sometimes I tiptoe out of bed
and listen. Make sure you're okay.
  You going to talk to her this time? Better had.

Steve Do you stop?

Sarah No. Chat me up. Come on, don't be a wuss.
  Hello. Say that. Hello. Go on, try it on me.

Steve Hello.

Sarah Ah, I'd go out with you.
  You've got to be more confident in yourself.

Steve I don't deserve someone like her.

Sarah Lots of people get things they don't deserve.

Steve Thanks.

Sarah 'S okay. What do you like about her? Apart from babies? Steve!

Steve She sings.

Sarah She sings?

Steve While she works, sort of to herself.

Sarah You sure she's not a monger?

Steve Sarah.

Sarah And would you?

Steve Would I what?

Sarah Give her one.

Steve Shut up.

Sarah You like her!
　Don't be scared.

　　Sarah holds out her hand. Steve passes her his phone.

Steve I won't leave you on your own.

Sarah I don't mind.

Steve I won't leave you. All right? You know that, don't you?

　　Sarah has changed the ringtone. She plays the new one. Steve takes his phone back.

Sarah John says I can get a place of my own.

Steve John says a lot of things.

Sarah Says he can put a word in.

Steve Have you taken your tic-tacs?

Sarah Have you taken yours?

Steve I don't need tic-tacs.

Sarah I could have a sunflower.

Steve Bloody hell.

Sarah I've always wanted my own sunflower. I'd water it and feed it.

Steve I'm going to have a word with John.

Sarah punches Steve on the arm.

Ow! Naughty. What?

Sarah With the light. You've got Dad's eyes.

FOUR

Soley's Bar.
  Late. She clears. Steve sits alone.

Soley We're closed. Time to go home. Everybody out.

Steve looks around to see who 'everybody' is – he is everybody. Soley prepares two glasses of a steaming drink.
  Steve stares at her. The moment passes. He makes his way out.

You don't want your drink?

Soley sets the drinks down at Steve's table. Steve joins her.

Skol!

She raises her glass, as does Steve.

Steve Skol.

They drink.

What is it?

Soley Black Death.

Steve nearly chokes on his drink.

Steve Doesn't that kill people?

Soley Mainly children. It's very strong, warming. And sweet, so kids like it. Back home, kids go out in the snow, drink it to keep warm, fall asleep. Don't wake up. Serves 'em right, curious little fuckers.

Steve What's Iceland like?

Soley Heaven. (*Beat.*) That was a joke, 's fucking boring.

Steve Heaven or Iceland?

Soley Iceland. Lots to do in Heaven.

Steve Sounds like Chessington.

Soley I tell jokes better in Icelandic. You want to hear one?

Steve I don't speak Icelandic.

Soley Details. (*Thinks.*) No, that's dirty. (*Thinks again.*) Ah! *Hvað gerirðu ef þú villist í íslenskum skógi?* [What do you do if you get lost in a forest in Iceland?'] And you say: *Ég veit það ekki, hvað gerirðu ef þú villist í íslenskum skógi?* [I don't know, what do you do if you get lost in a forest in Iceland?']

Steve repeats, clumsily.
Soley corrects him.
Steve repeats.

Good. *Stendur upp!* [Stand up.] (*Beat.*) If you knew Icelandic you'd be killing yourself. (*Beat.*) What's your name?

Steve Steve.

Soley Soley.

Steve I know.

Soley How?

Steve Soley's Bar.

Soley Sharp as a fox. How do you know I'm Soley?

Steve I don't.

Soley Well, I am. Old name, it means 'sun'.
  Now I teach you two things. So what do you teach me? Come on, first thing in your head?

Steve Dead arm.

Soley What?

Steve Nothing.

Soley No, you say 'dead arm'.

Steve No, it's –

Soley Tell me!

Steve I could teach you how to do a dead arm.

Soley What's a dead arm?
  Come on, soon we all die.

Steve You hit someone on the arm and it goes dead.

Soley You're fucking shitting me?

Steve Stupid.

Soley Crazy motherfucker, let's do it!

Steve Serious?

Soley Come on, pussy, show me!

Steve (*removing his jacket*) Well, you see, most people just sort of . . .

Soley Show me.
  You have good hands. Lots of marks, though, you fight? I upset you? Oh come on, big sensitive guy, show me.

Steve Most people sort of hit you there, like that, thumb on the outside. Now put your thumb through the middle, that's it . . . and it pushes the knuckle up and then you . . . hit the muscle with the knuckle . . . like that.

Soley Thumb on the inside.

Steve Yeah, that way if you hit someone, y'know, punch them. With your thumb on the outside. You'll probably break your own thumb but if you have your thumb on the inside it's more solid.

Soley I try on you.

Steve Okay.

Soley punches Steve, hard, on the bicep.

That was a good one.

Soley You're just saying that 'cause I'm a girl.

Steve No, it was good.

Soley Now you.
Come on, I don't break. Shit, you English. Come on.

Steve All right, just one.

Soley Wait. I put on my tough face. You see? Okay.

Steve gives Soley a dead arm.

Ow.

Steve Shit, you all right?
Sorry, I –

Soley wallops Steve on the arm.

That'll bruise.

Soley You got a bruise?

Steve I will do.

Soley I kiss it better.

She starts to rolls his sleeve up.

Steve (*stops her with the words*) I hurt people.

Soley Who doesn't?

Steve In my job.

Soley What job you do?

Steve I don't know. Mainly I deliver things.

Soley What kind of things?

Steve I don't ask. I just make sure people get what they want.

Soley Least it's not Starbucks. You ever hit a woman?

Steve Only dead arms.

Soley You hit me. I mean you *hit* me, I break your fucking head, okay?

Steve I will never hit you.

Soley I mean it.

Steve So do I.

Soley (*strokes his face*) Soft. Steve. Beautiful name.

Steve No one's said that before.

Soley Bet you say that to all the girls.

Steve No.

Soley You don't talk much. I like that. My last boyfriend talked all the time. Did my fucking head in.

Steve This . . . Did he hit you?

Soley Sometimes people get passionate. (*Beat.*) Tell me something.

Steve (*pause*) What?

Soley Anything?

Steve Oh, right, I thought you meant (what like?)

Soley Whatever your heart tells you.

Steve My heart?

Soley Don't think.

Steve You swear a lot.

Soley Tell me something I don't know.

Steve I'm not very good with words.

Soley Words are overrated.

Steve Your voice. When you sing. It's good.

She smiles and bites at the air, making Steve jump. She unbuttons Steve's sleeve, rolls it up neatly, revealing his bicep and a red mark. She strokes it.

Nice.

She kisses it, a lingering, sensual kiss.

Soley One thing.

Steve What's that?

Soley I'm a cat.
Meow. Now you. Now you.

Steve Meow?

Soley No. You're a dog.

Steve Woof?

Soley Dogs are stupid. But cats are clever. And we scratch.

Steve Ow.

Soley Scratch me.

Steve Dogs bite.

Soley Then bite me.

Soley leans in to Steve, offers him her neck. He bites her. She gasps. They stare at one another. She takes his hand.

So these the hands you work with.

Steve Yes.

She sucks one of Steve's knuckles.

Soley Right now, you can have anything in the world, what you ask for?

Steve A kiss.

They kiss.

Soley Now you ask me.

Steve What do you want?

Soley I want to take you upstairs, put on some music and fuck you till your eyes bleed.

Steve Okay.

FIVE

John's office.
  John, Sarah. John is her support worker. He stares blankly at a file.

Sarah He didn't get in till four, he thinks I don't know that but I do.

John Are you taking your medication?

Sarah Oblong one, round one, buh buh buh. God, you sound just like him, pair of right old ladies you two. You should form a club. An old ladies' club. You could sit knitting and moan about . . . socks.

Claire enters. She wears stylish glasses, her hair tied back.

Claire John. Really sorry to barge in, but with the conference accounts say the travel reqs have to be in now, we can't just buy tickets and claim back, they have to do it on account for some reason, do you want me / to put –

John I'm not going.

Claire Oh. You're not delivering?

John I need to spend time at home.

Claire Oh, nothing . . .

John Oh no no no.

Claire I could've done with a friend.

John Yeah.

Sarah Hello.

Claire Sorry, hi, I'm –

John Sarah, this is Claire, she's a colleague.

Claire Hi, Sarah, sorry, that was really rude of me.

Sarah I've seen you.

Claire And I've seen you. Hello, Sarah.

Sarah You're really pretty.

Claire Thank you. So are you.

Sarah I like your glasses.

Claire Thank you very much, Sarah, that's a lovely thing to say.

John Frame your face.

Claire Anyway, I'll see you later –

John Sure.

Sarah Bye.

Claire Bye, Sarah! Shit!

Claire drops a file. John helps gather papers.

John Here, let me.

Claire Sorry.

John It's all right.

Claire Such a muppet.

John No, no.

Claire Sorry.

Claire exits.

John What?

Sarah She's pretty.

John You were talking about your brother.

Sarah If I don't get some space of my own, I'm going to go properly mental. He won't bring girls home while I'm around and I need him to meet someone. And I can do it, I can. I can cook meals in the microwave and make tea and do shopping and clean and pay bills, I know all that. And I won't lose my keys, I'll be really careful. I just need a place of my own. So will you put me on the list?

John Sorry?

Sarah The list.
  For housing.
  You're thinking about that pretty lady, aren't you?

John No.

SIX

Meeting room.
  Nicola, her boss Chris (male), Dan and Ailsa.

Chris He said you used a particular word.

Nicola I called him a cunt.

  Dan flinches.

Ailsa I don't think we need to repeat / the word that was used.

Nicola If we're going to talk about what I said, we can say the word.

Chris Do you have any idea how offensive that word is, Nic?

Ailsa To women especially.

Nicola All women?

Ailsa Most women.

Nicola Did you ask round the office?

Chris It's not just women find it offensive, Nic.

Dan I find it offensive.

Chris It's actually a sexist term.

Nicola How can it be sexist for a woman to say / the word c—?

Dan Oh!

Chris It's using a woman's private parts as a term / of abuse.

Nicola Her what?

Ailsa Her private parts.

Chris I think we all know what private parts are.

Nicola Well, I'm sure your wife's relieved. Oh come on, you know what Derek's like.

Ailsa Yes, we all know what he's like, Nic, but you overstepped a boundary.

Nicola You're telling me you never use that word.

Ailsa No, I don't.

Nicola Chris?

Chris No.

Nicola You're telling me you never say the word –

Dan Ah!

Ailsa Can we please use an alternative?

Chris Perhaps for the purposes of this discussion we can use an alternative word.

Ailsa Why don't we just say 'the C word'?

Nicola I thought the 'C word' was cancer?

Dan No, it changed in the nineties.

Nicola How about 'crumble'?

Chris I don't see any problems with 'crumble', Ailsa?

Ailsa Crumble's fine.

Nicola Are you serious?

Chris Dan?

Dan I'm rather partial to crumble.

Nicola That's a little too much information.

Dan No, no, I mean the kind of crumble you eat, as opposed to . . . vagina.

Nicola I never had you down for a crumble eater.

Chris Nic, I get the feeling you're taking the piss.

Nicola So piss is acceptable?

Ailsa Oh for goodness sake.

Chris The point is, it's not acceptable to talk to a client the way you did.

Nicola But apparently making suggestive remarks about my private life is perfectly acceptable.

Chris He made suggestive remarks about your private life?

Nicola Yes.

Dan What did he say?

Nicola He asked me if I hadn't slept the night before.

Ailsa I'm sorry, I don't see –

Nicola It was the way he said it. It implied that I . . . Look, just forget it.

Chris We can't just forget it, this is the whole point of the meeting. Derek McMahon is a valued client.

Nicola Oh, so that's what this is about, the fact he brings us money is more important than –

Chris That's not what I said / and you know it.

Nicola – is more important than how he talks to me.

Ailsa From what I gather, your manner towards him was aggressive from the outset.

Chris Under the circumstances, I think asking if you hadn't slept was quite restrained of him, particularly given what you went on to say.

Nicola You don't have to deal with him – he makes these continual digs, this drip of remarks.

Dan What remarks?

Nicola It's the tone he uses.

Chris You're saying you called a customer a crumble because you didn't . . . because you didn't like his tone of voice?

Ailsa I'm getting a little tired of this.

Nicola Tired? Why, Ailsa? What were you doing last night?

Chris The point is, you can't call a client a woman's private parts. It's offensive.

Nicola So you're telling me there's something offensive about a woman's private parts?

Silence.

Dan (*confident*) Yes.

Chris No, we're not saying a woman's private parts are offensive.

Dan I mean no, sorry, strike that.

Chris Okay –

Nicola In that case, what's the problem?

Chris Okay, this meeting is over.

Chris rises to leave. Ailsa follows.

And wipe that grin off your face, you're acting like a child.

Nicola Don't talk to me like that, you wanker.

Chris Don't think I don't know how much time you spend pissing around on the internet. If you weren't so capable, you'd have been out months ago. So don't act like I'm some bad father or something. This is a job, not a playground for your personal crisis.

Chris and Ailsa leave.
Nicola holds her head in her hands.

Nicola I used to want to run my own clothes business.

Dan Sorry?

Nicola I used to have a life.

Dan Anything you want to talk about? Problems at home.

Nicola waves dismissively.

I'm a trained counsellor. Well, training.

Nicola Think I'll pass.

Dan Have you at least talked to someone close to you about this? 'John', is that your partner's name?

Nicola starts to laugh and cry at the same time.

Nicola Talk!
Guy I was at school with jacked his job in, he's walking to every country on earth. That's what I want to do.

Dan You want to walk to every country / on –

Nicola I mean I want to do something. I'm thirty. I'm supposed to have a baby or a mortgage or something. I don't even have a cat.

Dan Do you want a cat?

Nicola No, I hate cats. I'm not responsible for anything. I'm just the fucking madwoman in the office who cries all the time.
'Who's she?' 'The fucking madwoman.'

Dan How's your sex life?

Sorry, it's just last week we were learning how often when a couple have problems, it's the first thing to go. Fascinating course.

Nicola Sounds it.

Dan Sorry is that a bit personal?

Nicola It is a bit.

Dan No, you're right. It's just when Malcolm and me, I, me (I never remember which one it is, 'and me' or 'and . . .') Anyway, when we hit a sticky patch (so to speak) there were things that helped, if that makes sense.

Nicola Dan. The fuck are you talking about?

Dan How open-minded are you?

SEVEN

Park. Swings.
Steve, Soley. Dusk. The light fades during this scene.
Soley holds a balloon on a string.
Sarah returns with three identical ice lollies.

Sarah (*to Steve*) Yours melted.
Want to hear a secret?

Soley Okay.

Sarah I'm getting a place of my own soon.

Soley That's great.

Steve She's got this idea in her head she's moving out.

Sarah Steve, you're stifling my ambition.

Soley What's your ambition?

Sarah Pole-dancer.

Steve She's being silly.

Sarah With those things on your nips.

Soley Tassles.

Sarah Anyway, when I go, no one brings Steve lollies.

Steve Sarah.

Sarah Do you want to hear something funny? When Steve has bad dreams, he has to go outside and sit in his car.

Steve Stop showing off.

Sarah I'm going to have my own place, with my own sunflower. A really tall one.

Soley Well, if it's what you want, I think it's a good thing.

Sarah I like you.
  Steve made something for you. I wasn't supposed to say, but I reckon he's such a scaredy-cat, if I don't, he won't give it / to you.

Steve Sarah.

Sarah I'm going for a walk over there, bye.

  Sarah skips off. Soley is still holding Sarah's balloon.

Steve Don't go too far!

Sarah (*calling*) I will!

Soley So you made me a present?

Steve You shouldn't encourage her.

Soley Why not?

Steve She never lets anyone hold her balloon.

  Soley sings under her breath in Icelandic.

Soley You have bad dreams often?

Steve I don't sleep much, to be honest.

Soley 'I'm not you.' The other night, it's what you said. 'I'm not you'. Then you woke up. Then you left.

Steve I had to get back.

Soley I don't need to know what you do.

Steve I pick up a package. Normally from the same bloke. It's a bar in Soho. Girls on the door ask if you want a dance for twenty quid, you go in, sit down, they bring you a glass of champagne. Have your dance, then they charge you a hundred for the champagne. That sort of place. I collect parcels, packages, I make deliveries. DVDs, other stuff.

Soley I thought it was all online now.

Steve Online leaves a record. You can take stuff off your computer but it leaves a mark.

Soley Like a scar.

Steve Virtual is more permanent. DVD you can write over with no trace.

Soley No memory.

Steve My eyes are different to what most people's eyes are. I walk down the street and I see things you probably wouldn't see. I see opportunities that you probably wouldn't see, criminal opportunities. I see people doing things that you probably don't see. It's like it's imprinted on the back of my eyes, this . . . tape.

Soley We do what we have to.

Steve Now. This. Here. This is all that counts.

Soley Just start again. Like writing over a DVD?

Steve Yes.

Soley I don't know.

Steve Why?

Soley I'm a cat and you're a dog.

Steve takes a small packet from his pocket. He hands it to Soley. She unwraps it. It is a carved wooden cat, polished and completed.

Steve Something I do. When I was a boy . . .

Soley My mother used to tell me that objects like this, they carry the souls of unhappy people.

Steve Sounds like a fun lady.

Soley It's too much.

Steve Do you owe money?
   If you do –

Soley What makes you say that?

Steve If you do, you can tell me.

Soley Why do you say that?

Steve I hear you talking. I can help.
   Tell me.
   Please.

She touches his face.

Soley Steve.

Steve I love –

She withdraws her hand.

What?
   What?

Sarah enters.

EIGHT

Soley's Bar.
   Late. The bar is closed. Soley enters. The light comes on. Ralf wears a bandana and an early period New Wave of British Heavy Metal T-shirt.
   Soley carries the balloon from the park.
   Ralf holds aloft a banknote. Tucks it under the beer.

Ralf *Af hverju ertu svona sein?* [What kept you?]

   Ralf stands.
   Hard, discordant, black metal, and blurred, grainy pornographic film, like a flood.
   A series of tableaux. Soley and Ralf perform a dance of death.

NINE

John and Nicola's front room.
   The music morphs into the soundtrack to a porn film. As the scene begins, the soundtrack fades but can still be heard underneath.

Nicola And I've been eyeing you up all night, yeah?

John *(meaning the DVD)* Can we turn this off?

Nicola It's supposed to turn you on.

John It's just a bit full on, that's all.

   Nicola and John watch the DVD. Immediately they are transfixed by something extraordinary. They cock their heads to the side in unison, as if craning to get a better view of something. John flinches.

Bloody hell! I'm glad that wasn't in 3D.

Nicola John! We need to take this seriously.

John It's putting me off my stride.

Nicola Okay, just – (*She turns it off.*) Just do the character. Okay, I've been running up a tab and I haven't paid, all right?

John is miming something.

What are you doing?

John (*miming*) Cashing up.

Nicola What?

John I'm getting into character, like you said.

Nicola Just –

John What? It helps.

Nicola All right then, I've come in. (*She gestures for John to speak.*)

John It's time to close, Miss . . .?

Nicola Names aren't important, but you can call me Roxy.

John (*pause*) Sorry, my nan had a cat called Roxy.

Nicola 'S sake.

John Just, images, you know, don't want my nan's cat in my head when I'm trying to . . . That's just wrong, look, why can't I just call you Nic?

Nicola 'Cause it's a fantasy. Look, call me . . . Amber or something – do you have any pets called Amber?

John No.

Nicola Fine. Ask me to settle up.

John So I'm afraid I'm going to have to ask you to settle up, Amber, I'm closing.

Nicola Sure, I'll – oh. I've forgotten my purse. I can't pay. Not in cash, anyway.

John Have you got a card?

Nicola They're all in my purse.

John Well, you seem trustworthy. Tell you what, you can settle up next time you're in.

Nicola I'm only in town for one night. I won't ever be here again – I have to pay now.

John I'll write down the address, then you can send me the . . .

Have you got any other methods of payment, any . . . other things?

Nicola Well, I'm sure we can think of something, Mr . . .

John Hasselhoff. Barry Hasselhoff.

Nicola John!

John Who's John? I'm Barry.

Nicola You can't have that name.

John What's wrong with it?

Nicola Hasselhoff? It's fucking David –

John It's a name, it's not like David Hasselhoff's the only one with that name.

Nicola How many other Hasselhoffs do you know?

John Just the one.

Nicola Who?

John Barry Hasselhoff.

Nicola Stop making jokes.

John It's a little hard.

Nicola At least something is.

John That's cheap.

Nicola Can we just try and do this.

John I'm sorry. It's late, and I'm tired. I've got to be at work in the morning.

Nicola huffs.

Tell me what you want me to do.

Nicola I want you to be passionate about me. Push me onto the sofa, tear my clothes off, fuck me like an animal.

John You're not an animal, you're a woman.

Nicola I'm after a fuck, not a lecture.

John I can't just fuck you like an animal. I need a bit of a wind-up.

Nicola The whole point of fucking someone like an animal is that it doesn't need 'a bit of a wind-up'. It's supposed to be spontaneous.

John This is hardly spontaneous. Look, this whole stranger in a bar thing just doesn't do it for me.

Nicola Well then, what? What's your fantasy? And don't say a threesome because we're not doing that.
You were going to say a threesome, weren't you?

John I was not.

Nicola Is that what you want, a threesome?

John No.

Nicola Do you want me to put my thumb up your arse?

John Why would I want you to do that?

Nicola I read it was nice.
How about I'm your sexy boss and I'm making you work late?

John How about you're my secretary?

Nicola You want to be the boss?

John Okay.

Nicola Hang on.

John Where are you going?

Nicola exits.

Nicola (*off*) What do you want to call me?

John Something plain.

Nicola (*off*) Jane.

John How about Claire?

Nicola enters, wearing stylish glasses, hair tied back, carrying a folder.

Nicola It's me. Claire. I've got the photocopying you asked for. (*She drops the folder.*) Whoops. Silly!

She bends down, rubbing into him as she does so.

My. I can see why you're the boss.

She turns around.

I always find working late so stressful. How do you cope?

She strokes his crotch.

My. I guess that's what they call executive class.
Perhaps I can help you unwind.

She unzips his fly.

Fuck me. Fuck me with your fat cock.

John All right.

They move apart.

Nicola What? What?

John The way you're acting, it's embarrassing.

Nicola Embarrassing?

John Yes.

Nicola You think I'm cheap.

John No.

Nicola When we go out for a meal, you always order the house wine.

John The fuck did that come from? How long have you been storing that up in your little book?

Nicola What little book?

John Your book of things to bring up in an argument. How come you can't replace a DVD in its box but you file this shit away?

Nicola It would be nice to feel like I'm more than house wine. You know, I'd like to be a nice bottle of Rioja or something.

John This is unbelievable.

Nicola Is there someone else?

John What?

Nicola Who's Claire?

John No one.

Nicola You've mentioned a Claire. Someone at work, did I meet her at Christmas, I fucking did, that –

John Oh for goodness sake, yes, there's a Claire at work. There's a Jane too and you said Jane.

Nicola Is that who you're seeing? When you work late?

John This is ridiculous.

Nicola Oh, I'm ridiculous now.

John How dare you? Just because I don't want to have sex right now, it doesn't mean I'm . . . Does it not occur to you that you're the problem?

Nicola What?

John It's like living with a stranger. I don't know who you are. This thing at work.

Nicola I am under a lot of stress.

John sighs.

Don't do that! I know you think my job's a piece of shit but we / can't all . . .

John Whoa, when did I say that?

Nicola We can't all be saving the fucking world.

John Don't have a go at me 'cause you hate your job Nic, I don't make you do it, yeah? If you don't want to do it, don't. Yeah, as it happens, I don't think it's great, I can't help that. But you want to earn more money, that's fine. I'm allowed to think that. But don't act like I think I'm, y'know, that I (where are you going?)

Nicola Need a drink.

Nicola exits. She returns with a bottle of cider.

John What's got into you?

Nicola Me? You're the one's turned into some uptight smug . . . wombat.

John Wombat?

Nicola All right, wrong animal, big fucking deal. I'm so stupid and you're so clever.

John Don't do that!

Nicola When I touch you it's like you think I'm dirty.

John Well, that's hardly surprising.

Nicola You fucking –
  Do you want to break up?

John Sorry.

Nicola Do you want to break up?

John I'm sorry, I shouldn't have said that.
  I don't know.
  Maybe we need some space.
  Maybe I should go to the conference.
  It might be good for both of us.

Nicola Will Claire be there?

John I'll sleep in the spare room.

Nicola Fine.

  John starts to leave.

John.

  He turns.

While you're up there, go fuck yourself.

TEN

Soley's Bar.
  Late evening. Peter and Steve sit, separately. Peter dressed as before. Empty shot glasses. Laptop. He tries to construct a card house, but is too drunk.

A Barman is on the phone, talking dirty, in English. Occasionally this becomes apparent.

Peter Hong Kong.
China.
Malaysia.
Thailand, ladyboys and Singapore slings in Singapore.
Philippines (shoes).
Australia (All Blacks! No, that's New Zealand).
New Zealand.
Samoa . . . what comes after Samoa?
What comes after Samoa?

Steve is staring at Peter.

Sorry. Sorry mate, sorry. I won't . . .

Peter mimes zipping up his lips. He rises and moves towards Steve.

It's Steve, right? Isn't it? Barman, more drinks. Friends, shake hands. C'mon, shake hands.

Steve approaches the Barman, stares.

Took your advice. Went to see her. Begged me to come back. Embarrassing ('barrassing).

Steve Excuse me.

Peter Told her I'm off. Round the world. Dad was in tears, horrible, begged me to take her back.

Steve Excuse me.

Barman (*into phone, continuing.*) Are you touching it now? How does it feel? Does it – *hang on.*

The Barman looks up at Steve.

Steve You said she'd be an hour. (*Beat.*) It's been an hour.

Barman I told you she might be an hour. (*Into phone.*) Describe it? Like a chihuahua fresh out the pond?

40

Steve Did she not say anything?

Peter Tonga!

Barman No.

Peter That's what's after Samoa.

Barman Ralf asked me to mind the bar.

Steve Who's Ralf?

Barman If you want to wait, she might turn up.

Peter Lot of bitty islands.

Barman Nothing else I can do, mate.

Peter Fiji and the other one.

Barman (*next few lines spoken looking directly at Steve*) Tell me what you're thinking about. Really? *Really?* Yeah. Not a stitch. Like a girder (*hang on*) –
 Mate, you can stare all you like, I don't know when she's coming back, she didn't say. What part of 'don't know' don't you understand?

Steve I shouldn't have given her the cat.
 It was too much.

Barman (*into phone*) No, hang on darlin', I'm still here. (*To Steve.*) What fucking cat?

Steve Is she in trouble, can you tell me that?

Barman (*into phone*) Sorry, no, just some mad cunt taking the piss. So where are you now?

 Steve grabs the Barman's head and slams it down on the counter. He holds it there. Peter is transfixed.

Steve That's not a nice word.

Barman No.

Steve I'm going to go and sit over there and wait.

Barman Yeah.

Steve lets the Barman go and begins to return to his stool. Steve takes his seat. Pause. He gets up and returns to the Barman, quietly intense. A long pause. No one moves.

Steve That wasn't me. That was someone else.

Steve takes his seat again. A pause.

Peter Barman, a drink for my friend. What you having, beer? Whisky? Whisky for my friend. (*To Steve.*) So we're talking, the three of us, me, Rachel and Dad. And it's all amicable. And he goes to the side, my dad, to make a cup of tea, and I'm staring at his neck, the skin on the back of his neck, the hair, and something in me snaps.

The Barman brings a whisky.

Barman On the house, mate.

The Barman returns to the bar, makes another call, starts talking softly. We can't hear what he's saying until the end of the scene.

Peter And I think. I'm not having this. So I pounce. He's trying to shake me off and Rachel's in a tizzy but I'm clinging on like a monkey, a monkey rucksack, and I won't let go. And he's tiring, I can feel his knees going, not quickly, just sort of like, errhhh, with a groan. And before I know it he's curled up in a little ball like a Cumberland sausage and I'm pummelling his arse with my fists and there's blood, Rachel's screaming, but I don't stop. I can't. And he's not moving. You understand me. I killed him. I killed him dead.

Steve rises to leave.

You don't believe me, do you? Do you?

He was supposed to protect me. He stole her from me. My own dad. You don't know what that's like.

Steve Go home.

Peter Haven't got a home.

Steve Get some sleep.

Peter If I wanted someone to not be alive any more, how much would that cost?
  I've got money.

Steve That's not me.

Peter It is.

Steve You've made a mistake. You've mistaken me for someone else.

Peter It's in your eyes.

Steve What is?

Peter I've got money.

Steve What's in my eyes?

Peter I can see it now.

Steve There's nothing in my eyes.

Peter How much would it cost?

Steve These are my eyes. No one else's.

Peter I got money from the business. I swear.
  Tell me what to do.
  I've got so much anger in me. Sometimes I don't know what to do with it.

Steve Go home. Have a shave. Have a wash. Get some sleep. Talk to your mates or something.

Steve exits.

Peter My mates. Yeah, I got lots of friends.

Peter opens his laptop and logs on. As the light from the screen lights him up, we hear the Barman again.

Barman . . . and I'd put my hands on your hips. And you'd put your hands on the counter. And I'd sniff your neck, and –

ELEVEN

Hotel bar.
Late. John and Claire, on their second bottle.

John We do it every day and don't give it a second thought, that's the point. Someone can't pay their bills and we're programmed to think it's because of their learning difficulties, 'cause that's *who they are*, they're a person with learning difficulties, but maybe it's just that they're lazy – no, I'm serious!

Claire I'd love to see Jenny's face if she heard you say that. 'Maybe it's just that they're lazy.'

John Not all of them, but some of them. Some people with learning difficulties are lazy. Some people are lazy full stop. Some people are just thick. Just because you've got learning difficulties doesn't mean you're thick but it doesn't stop you from being a pig ignorant fuckwit either.

Claire You can't say that!

John We do this all the time, we have this tendency to give people this redemption story that just isn't there.

Claire It's not just work, it's the media.

John (Maybe redemption's strong.)

Claire I think you're on to something (I don't think it is). I mean that's what depression is, isn't it, an inability to

44

see the bad things that happen to you as being random, that instead it's a product of a narrative –

John The narrative being that you're a bad person.

Claire Yes.

John Fuck, we've solved depression!

Claire Hallelujah.
  You're brilliant, John, you're brilliant but you're mad.

John It's the only sane reaction to this place.

Claire What is, being mad?

John It's like overhearing someone on the bus and you can't help it – what their background is, what kind of school they went to, how their relationship is going –

Claire Yeah.

  John's phone.

John I thought this was off, sorry.

Claire Do you need to . . . ?

John No, it's a, I don't know the number.

Claire Probably a client.

John Leave me alone, you fuckers, I'm having a drink.

  John sends it to voicemail.

Sorry.

Claire Penny.

John Mm? Oh, just . . .

Claire (*of the wine*) This is good. Worth pushing the boat out.

John Yeah.

Claire (*pouring*) How are things with Nic?

John Oh God, you'll have to top me up. It's . . . Do you mind talking about this?

Claire No, no, God, if it helps.

John I don't want to be a burden.

Claire No no no no no. No. No!

John It's like we met at university and she was so passionate about the environment and global warming, she was for ever organising fundraising and awareness-raising things and she had so much energy and I found that . . . attractive or . . .

Claire Sure.

John And then after uni she was going to work for Amnesty or whatever (you sure you don't mind me?) but she decided to get some experience marketing in the private sector, thought it would look good on her CV and . . . maybe she got used to the money or . . .

Claire No chance of that with us.

John It's no longer a stepping stone, it's what she does. I think she gave up on her dreams. She doesn't have any dreams, that's what I'm trying to say . . . See, I'm not actually sure it was the right-on stuff that she liked, I think it was the hanging out and the fun and organising things, really.

Claire That's quite patronising.

John No no, it's just that it happened to be that stall she stopped at in freshers' week rather than the rugby stall. I honestly think that. It's like living with a stranger. You can know someone so well and at the same time . . .

Claire Not know them at all.

John (*beat*) I hate these things.

Claire Yeah.

John All the milling around, name tags.

Claire Yeah, I noticed you wrote 'Bob' on yours.

John Well, I just got tired of people coming up to me and . . . Something about the atmosphere at these places, I don't know. I saw this programme, this documentary on More Four about –

Claire I love More Four.

John Yeah . . . this documentary about swingers, and you'd expect it would be all glamorous and stylish and . . . but the reality is, it's so . . .

Claire Mmmm.

John . . . mundane, you know?

Claire Yeah.

John It's . . .
  Fuck.

Claire What?

John You know they design these places to make you forget about the real world, they position the bars and what-not so you can't see the way out. Gives you the illusion of being trapped.

Claire Is that how you feel?

John (*pause*) Delegates. What a weird word.

Claire I'm not even so sure our lives are stories. Or not very good ones, they go on too long, they don't make sense, you get dead ends, things happen in the wrong order, you only find sense 'cause that's what you're looking for, it's not there!

John I guess not.

Claire We're animals, there's no grand narrative. But strip away this bullshit that it all *means* something . . . and we're astonishing . . . All we are is who we are right now.

They kiss. They move apart. They kiss again.

John We shouldn't do this.

Claire moves away gently.

Claire You're with someone. So am I. But this is something else. If you want it to be.

John Okay.

Claire Yeah?

John Yeah.

Claire Okay.

TWELVE

Soley's Bar. Late.
Nicola and Peter at the same table. Full glasses of wine next to them and a half-opened bottle of Rioja. Napkins. A bowl of olives, nearly empty. They are drunk.
Peter is looking smart. He has made an effort.
Soley is on the phone, speaking in English.

Peter How many people do you have to bite to be a vampire mistress?

Nicola A lot.

Peter I don't know where you get the time.

Nicola God, nothing else to do at work apart from become a vampire mistress.

Peter I thought running your own business would be quite time-consuming.

Nicola (*beat*) Oh yeah, well, yeah, of course, the business, yeah, but there's, well, you know how it is.

Peter You're just moaning, aren't you?

Nicola Yeah!

Peter Your own fair trade clothing business. I'm so pleased for you, you've done so well. I mean most people –

Nicola I know, I know.

Peter They've done nothing.

Soley (*continuing, on the phone*) I can't.

Nicola Yeah, yeah.

Peter But you, I mean, God.

Soley No, Steve, I have to go.

Nicola Exactly.

Soley I said I have to go.

Peter You've not sold out, taken the easy option.

Nicola It's true, yes.

Soley I'm sorry.

Soley slams the phone down. Takes a moment to compose herself. Looks at accounts. Slams the book shut, exits out back. She looks like she is about to cry.

Nicola She's so beautiful.

Peter So are you.

Nicola Are you flirting?

Peter Consider it a poke.

Nicola Well, I might just have to poke you back.

Peter Your own label. Wow.

Soley reappears from out back, composed.

Nicola 'Nother one?

Peter Oh bollocks, we're still young, aren't we?

Nicola We've still got it, haven't we?

Peter We bloody have!

Nicola More Rioja!

Peter Soley, another bottle of Rioja, please!

Nicola Sometimes you've just got to say fuck it, haven't you?

Peter I'll drink to that. Cheers!

Nicola Fuck it!

Peter Fuck it!

They drink.

Nicola Do you ever imagine you're part of some big James Bond international conspiracy, that everything that went wrong in your life is the result of unseen dark forces, and not just that you're, y'know, a bit shit?

Peter Yeah.

Nicola I always think that. Better than taking responsibility, isn't it?

Peter Thanks for the poke.

Nicola Thanks for being my friend.

Peter I needed one, what with . . .

Nicola I know, it's so tragic, about your wife.

Peter Yeah.

Nicola Just . . . awful . . . dying like that. And there was a history of it?

Peter Death?

Nicola The heart condition.

Peter Mmmm.

Nicola And so suddenly. Rachel, you said?

Peter Yeah.

Nicola This last few years must have been awful.

Peter So your partner's at a conference?

Nicola Oh God, yeah, he's saving the world. In Birmingham. Thinks he's Mother Teresa.

Peter He's not dead, though.

Nicola Only from the waist down. Fuck him, he's not ruining my night. Tell me about your travel plans, I think it's amazing, I really do.

Peter Do you?

Nicola The world needs a bit of madness – God, all this sanity, it drives me round the bend, the ambition of it, I love it! You're so . . . You know where you're going. Can I come? Ha ha, only joking (I'm not actually).

Soley brings the bottle to the table and opens it.

Ahhh!

Attached to her waiter's friend is a key chain from which hangs the carved wooden cat. During the following, she pours a glass each.

Ohh, I love your cat.

The bar phone rings.

It's gorgeous, where did you get it?

Soley A friend.

Nicola Did she make it?

Soley You like it?

Nicola It's gorgeous.

Soley You have it.

Soley removes the cat from her waiter's friend and hands it to Nicola.

Nicola Oh I can't, it's too much.

Soley You like it, take it.

Nicola Let me give you / something for –?

Soley On the house.

Nicola That's so lovely of you, thank you.

Soley returns to the bar. The phone continues to ring for about ten seconds. Peter and Nicola watch Soley as she ignores it. It rings off.

(*Mouths.*) So lovely.

Peter That is, it's . . . lovely.

Nicola I love Rioja, all yummy on my tongue.

The phone goes. Soley answers.

Soley I told you not to call.

She takes the phone out back.

Nicola She's so unhappy. Do you ever feel scared you haven't done enough?

Peter Yes.

Nicola About a week ago, I had a dream where every time I ever did anything or went anywhere or said anything, people would say: 'Someone else just did that, you're just copying them, aren't you?' Turns out I never had a single original thought my whole life. How scary is that?

Peter That's funny. I had that dream too.

Nicola Tell me something. I want to hear something I've never heard before, something new, something fresh.

Peter What like?

Nicola Anything at all.

Peter God, something new . . . I really don't, ah! Mm, it's a bit . . .

Nicola Spit it out!

Peter When you observe the world at the smallest level, I mean tiny – atoms exist as both waves and particles, and they have entirely different structural patterns, but you only get to see them when you look for them . . . I'm not explaining this very well –

Nicola No no.

Peter In order to see the atoms as a wave you have to shine light on them in a certain way and the wave is there, but you can't see the particles. Or you can choose to see the atoms as particles but you can't see it as waves at the same time . . . God, you know this!

Nicola Do I?

Peter God told us this.
   After school, don't you remember?

Nicola God, yes. God!
   And there was a cat, what was that cat, I'm remembering it all now. What? What are you looking at me like that for?

Peter You look so alive.

Nicola What was the cat?

Peter That guy, what was his name, Stringer or something, he had this way of, it's like a cat in a box with a cyanide capsule, and the cat is both dead and alive at the same time.

Nicola Sounds like me. Sorry, do you mind me touching your leg?

Peter No.

Nicola Carry on.

Peter It's been quite a long time since I've been touched by a woman.

Nicola Are you sure you don't mind?

Peter No. I mean, no, I don't mind. It's really nice.

Nicola Will you carry on talking?

Peter That's pretty much it.

Nicola Please just carry on talking.

Peter Well, the idea is that you don't know whether the cat is alive or dead until you . . . that's really nice.
  It's been a long time since I've been touched by a woman.

Nicola Just carry on talking.

Peter Until you open the box and look.

Nicola Yeah.

Peter And so until you open the box the cat is alive and dead at the same time . . .

Nicola Carry on.

Peter It's been so long.

Nicola It's okay.
Fuck, I've spilt something, I'm so sorry.
Well, there's my glass and that's –

Pause.

Is that? But I only got to the top of your thigh.

Peter I'm leaking on the table.

Nicola Let me get you a napkin, quick before she comes back.

Nicola tries to clean Peter with a napkin, frantically.
Soley appears from out back.

Soley What the fuck is going on?

Peter Nothing we just spilt something.

Soley (*pulls at the tablecloth*) What the fuck is this?

Nicola Nothing, nothing, he's just upset about his wife.

Soley Were you jerking him off?

Nicola No.

Soley You better not be jerking him off.

Nicola No, no, he just needs some space.

Soley There's no jerking off in here. I know we don't have a sign but it's definitely a rule, okay? (*Beat.*) Don't move.

Soley exits out back.

Nicola Fuck was I thinking?

Peter My wife's not dead. She left me for my dad. I want to see her but I'm too scared. Such a cunt.

Nicola God.

Peter Please help me.

Nicola I'm so sorry.

Nicola leaves. Soley emerges from the back with cloth and bucket.

Soley Hey!

Soley looks at the drunken, shaking Peter. She cleans him up.

Peter Bill please, Soley.

Peter notices that Nicola has left the cat. He picks it up. He removes a credit card from his wallet, puts it down on the table.

Soley This is extra.

Soley takes Peter's card, returns to the bar and starts to process the bill.
The city speaks. An awesome, merciless noise.
Peter pushes the bowl along the table, slowly, deliberately, until it rests precariously on the side of the table. He pushes it as far as it can possibly go without falling.
The noise reaches its apex. Something terrible.
Soley sees something out the window and instead of leaving the bill on Peter's table, she continues past, shocked. Peter pushes the bowl a final time.
Blackout.

Part Two

THIRTEEN

Soley's.
  John, Peter. Late afternoon.

John How much?

Peter I think it was sixteen quid.

John No, how much did you drink?

Peter Oh um. Two or three –

John Glasses?

Peter Bottles.

John You had three bottles –

Peter I know –

John Of sixteen-pound Rioja.

Peter I think so.

John Where were you sat?

Peter Here.

John Where exactly?

Peter I was here and she was kind of here.

John Did you eat anything?

Peter Some olives.

John Green or black?

Peter Mixed. Sort of spicy.

  Soley brings a coffee and a beer to the table.

Soley (*to Peter*) I'm sorry about your girlfriend. These are on the house.

She returns to the bar.

Peter I was a few years above her at school. Nothing weird, I mean only a few years.
She moved away, her stepdad got some –

John Glenn.

Peter Yeah, that's right, he got some work in Hungerford or somewhere.

John And how did you get in touch again – she poked you or whatever?

Peter Well, bit me.

John She what?

Peter Bit me. She turned me into a . . . vampire.
She was a vampire mistress and it's what you do, you bite people. Do you use Facebook?

John No.

Peter You know how poking works?

John I think so, you poke someone you fancy.

Peter No no, you don't have to fancy someone.

John Someone told me it meant that really it means you fancy someone.
So she was a vampire mistress.

Peter It's just a bit of fun.

John But she bit you.

Peter Yeah.

John And what did that make you?

Peter A rockstar vampire.

I'm sorry, this probably sounds a bit weird and inappropriate.

John Oh no.

Why does the waitress think she was your girlfriend?

Peter I don't know, we were here together.

John I mean, was there anything that might have made her think she was your girlfriend?

Peter I was just pleased to hear from her. I was at quite a low point. Drinking. I had ideas. My wife left me for my dad. It was just nice that she was doing so / well.

John Hang on, your wife left you for your dad?

Peter I'd rather not (it was very painful. It still is.) Look, what I was saying is, I was pleased to hear that things were going so well for Nic – you know, with her business and everything?

John *Her* business?

Peter Yeah, the fairly-traded stuff.

John What fairly-traded stuff?

Peter Fairly-traded clothes. You know, her business.

John She didn't have a business.

Peter She did.

John I'd know if she had a business.

Peter It's on her profile (she told me all about it). On Facebook you have a profile, you know, stuff about you, and she talks about her business.

John How do you read this?

Peter You need to be her friend. It's just how it works.

John She worked in marketing for an advertising company. They have the contract for the buses.

She was about to be sacked for calling someone a . . . rude word.

Did she talk about me?

Peter Yeah.

John What did she say?

Peter She said you, um, work in social work. She said you were very good at your job. She said she loved you.

John She said that?

Peter Yeah.

John When you called the other day . . . I checked my incoming calls and . . . that night you called.

Peter Oh no, that was Nic. I think the impact damaged her phone. She said she wanted to talk to you. So I dialled on my phone but just went to voicemail.

Peter removes the carved wooden cat from his jacket pocket. He hands it to John. When Soley sees this, she stops her work and watches the two men.

She left this. Soley there had it on a key ring, and Nic liked it, so she gave it to her. She forgot it.

John turns it over in his hands, stares at it. He looks at Soley. Then back at the cat.
Soley exits out back.

I don't know what else to say.

Peter starts to leave. He stops.

She didn't say she loved you. She said she didn't know if you cared about her any more. I'm sorry. If it was me –

John Yeah well, it's not, is it?

Anything else I should know? Vampires or any other secrets?

Steve enters. He takes a seat. As he passes Peter, the two men realise they know each other from somewhere.

Peter I wish it was me. Who died.

John Me too.

Peter exits.
John plays with the cat. Steve watches this. John glances over at Steve. John leaves money, stands.
Soley enters.

Steve All right.

John Hi.

John leaves.

Soley You know him?

Steve Sarah's support worker. Looks like she's in good hands.

Soley makes Steve a tea.

S'pose you've seen me. Standing under the street lamp like a lemon. Old Bill moved me on a couple of times.
It's okay.
Actually it's not (thank you).
I wake up in the night. Dreams.
That night, I felt safe.
Pain in my chest like when you eat your tea too quick.
You in trouble?
I can help.
Is he the one who hit you?

Soley You don't know Ralf.

Steve You think I'm scared of a bloke called Ralf? He's got a mullet.

Soley Knight in shining armour, aren't you?
  If you knew about me.

Steve I do know about you.

Soley Who I was.

Steve That doesn't matter.

Soley I owe money.

Steve How much?

Soley No –

Steve How much?

*Soley fetches a well-worn handwritten piece of paper.
She hands it to Steve. He takes some glasses from his
pocket. He reads the note. He replaces his glasses.*

What about the bar?

Soley It's a lease.

Steve I thought you'd always been here.

Soley Feels like it.

Steve Let me help.

A long pause.

Why not?

Soley I'm scared.

Steve I'll protect you.

Soley Not just Ralf.

Steve You're not scared of me.

Soley Some people think they have chemistry, but really
it's just friction. I'm a cat and you're a dog, remember?

Steve That's just something we say.

Soley Ralf was my boyfriend. He used to invite his friends round. To have sex with me. I was thirteen, fourteen. He still his videotapes.

Steve What abou the coppers?

Soley One time a boy got stabbed. I stabbed him.
  He wants me to go back with him.

Steve To Iceland.

Soley Says he'll forget about the debt.

Steve No.

Soley Don't come near me.

Steve I love you.

  Soley laughs hysterically.

Soley Get the fuck away from me!

Steve No.

Soley Go away. (*She slaps him.*) Go away. (*Slaps him.*) Go away go away go away. (*Slaps him.*) Cunt!

Steve Don't call me that.

Soley You thought about it, didn't you? Thought about hitting me. Why don't you, Steve, why don't you hit me?

Steve Why are you doing this?

  Peter enters.

Soley Because I hate you and I never want to see you again.

Peter Sorry, I think I left my phone, do you mind if I –?

  Peter scouts round near the bar.

Sorry, let me just –
  Could you ring it for me?

Soley It's not a good time.

Peter It's got all my numbers.

Steve She said it's not a good time.

Peter Please. I just need this one thing not to go wrong.

Soley What's your number?

Steve I've got it.

Steve takes Peter's card from his pocket. He dials the number. A phone rings. Everyone looks around. Peter pats his pockets. Finds it.

Soley What's that in your hand? Is that a knife?

Peter Thanks.

Peter exits.
  Steve and Soley stare at one another.
  Black metal, blurred pornographic images.
  The music fades

FOURTEEN

Kitchen.
  Peter and Rachel.

Rachel How d'you get in?

Peter Key.

Rachel I know, I mean I thought you gave me your key.

Peter Kept one.

Rachel Your dad'll be back soon.

Peter Will he?

Rachel Yeah.

Peter He normally has a meeting this time. Always used to.

Rachel It changed.

Peter Why, isn't this convenient?

Rachel Not really.

Peter Why?

Rachel You're drunk.

Peter I thought we could have a chat.

Rachel About what?

Peter Us.

Rachel This really isn't a good time.

Peter You're so cold to me. After the way you treated me.

Rachel exits. She returns with a sheaf of papers.

Rachel Pick one. Any one.

Peter What are they?

Rachel Just pick one.

Peter Tell me what they are.

Rachel I'll pick one. (*Reads.*) 'You are a disease, a sickness, a disgusting abomination, the pair of you make me vomit, I wish you were corpses, rotting corpses so I could piss on you and then shit . . .'
Pages and pages.

Peter What is it?

Rachel It's from your email.

Peter Someone stole my computer.

Rachel Months of this.

You don't know what you were like. You were all right on the medication. What did you expect?

Peter Not that you'd end up shagging my dad.

Rachel He was kind to me.

Peter Remember thinking how kind he was. Thinking it was a good thing (he needed the company. Both of you.)

Rachel We did.

Peter So you abandoned me?

Rachel Only when I couldn't cope.

Peter Did you ever love me?

Rachel I think so.

Peter I wish he was dead.

Rachel You've made that very clear.

Peter Maybe I'll do something about it.

Rachel We both know that's not true.

Peter turns to conceal the knife he removes from his pocket.

Peter That river bank in Issan? Our honeymoon? Rach? The collapsed pier, drinking local wine with too strong camembert, I can taste the pepper. You wanted to make love but I said no 'cause there were kids around.

Rachel There weren't kids around.

Peter There were. But that's you and me, isn't it? One of us thinks about responsibility, the other doesn't.
I wish we had now.
Why do I have to forget you?

Rachel Call your dad, he wants to talk to you. Properly, not abuse.

Peter What are we going to do? Compare notes?

Rachel We understand this is messy, but if you continue harassing me and your dad then / we'll have –

Peter His name's Tony. Don't say 'your dad'. That's what Mum would say. You're not my mum.

Rachel Please go.

Peter That's all you've got to say?

Peter grimaces. Facing away from Rachel, he replaces the knife in his pocket.

Rachel What?

Peter At least shake hands. Come on. Shake on it.

Peter takes his hand from his jacket pocket, extends it, palm down.

Then I'll go.

Rachel shakes.

Rachel My God!

She tries to withdraw her palm, but Peter grips it tight.

Peter I killed someone. A girl. We went on a date. And I killed her.

Rachel pulls free. She has blood on her hands. Peter's blood. Peter raises his palms.

Blood on my hands. Now you have too.

Peter leaves.

FIFTEEN

John's office.
  John, Sarah, Steve.

Sarah I want my own sunflower.

Steve I'll get you a sunflower.
  You can have one at home, darling.

Sarah I still love you, Steve, I just can't live with you any more.

Steve She doesn't know what she means.

John I have to say your behaviour is quite controlling.

Steve Controlling?
  Controlling?

John I think you need to calm down.

Sarah Steve, take a deep breath.

Steve Why is everyone telling me I'm not calm?

John Everyone isn't –

Steve I'm perfectly calm. Only thing's winding me up is you two.

John Sarah is more capable than you give her credit for.

Steve The other day she burnt herself.

John What?

Sarah I was doing the ironing.

Steve See.

John Everyone burns themselves doing the ironing. Have you ever burnt yourself doing the ironing?

Steve No.

Sarah That's 'cause you never do the ironing.

Steve Look.

Sarah Get off me.

Steve Look at that.

John I think you're hurting her.

Steve No I'm not.

Sarah Ow.

John You need to let go of her arm.

Sarah Steve, it hurts.

Steve Stop making such a fuss. What's your problem? You're living in cloud cuckoo land. She can't live on her own. Look at her!.

Sarah You're the stalker.

Steve What?

Sarah That girl doesn't want to see him any more.

Steve You talk to him about her?

Sarah He keeps hanging round her house all the time.

Steve You talk about me?

Sarah I've heard him on the phone.

Steve You shouldn't listen to people's phone calls.

John Okay.

Claire enters.

Sarah You sit in the car right outside my window.

Steve Will you shut your stupid mouth? Fucking fifteen years I looked after you, fifteen years. People thought I was weird. Steve and his mong sister. The amount I've given up for you. Everything I do is for you, and this is how you repay me.

John I think there's been a –

Steve Maybe Dad was right. Maybe you are just a spastic.

Don't you look at me like that. You've no idea. You people. It just doesn't affect you, does it? Life. It's all just work.

Claire Everything okay?

John We're fine. Thanks, Claire.

Claire exits.

Steve I'm sorry. I'm calm now.

John I'm going to have to ask you to leave.

Steve I said I'm calm.

Pause.

You coming?

Sarah No.

John I think she's staying here.

Steve I'm not talking to you. Come on. I'll buy you a lolly.

Sarah I don't want a lolly. I'm not a child. And you're not my dad. So stop acting like him.

Steve exits.

Steve.

John Sarah. (*Beat.*) I think it's your brother needs taking care of, not you.

Sarah I've never seen him like that.

John sighs. He picks up the carved wooden cat. He toys with it, turning it over in his hands.

You've got to move on, haven't you?

John What?

Sarah Can't keep holding on to things. That's what you said.

John How dare you?

Sarah Sorry.

John How dare you talk to me like that? Who do you think you are to tell me to move on? How dare you?

Sarah I was talking about Steve.

Pause.

He makes those.

John What?

Sarah Your cat. He makes them when he's angry. He used to do it when Dad was being naughty. Where'd you get yours?

SIXTEEN

Out in the suburbs. An underpass by the river. Night.
Steve, Peter. There is a case on the walkway. Steve is pointing a gun at Peter.

Steve Any last words?

Peter Don't shoot me in the bollocks.

Steve Those are your last words?

Peter I just mean don't miss, you know, don't maim me. It's more the pain than the death I'm afraid of. I don't want to be a viral.

Steve What?

Peter Funny email goes round offices.

He raises the gun.

Hang on.

Steve Fucking hell, I was about to do it.

Peter I just need a moment.

Steve What for?

Peter Make sure I'm doing the right thing. Kind of permanent this, isn't it?
Sorry, I'm just going through the pros and cons of me being around. Can't think of too many pros. That's probably a good sign, isn't it?

Steve Do you want me to do this or not?

Peter Yes. Definitely. No, wait.

Steve You're doing my nerves.

Peter Come on, let's do it.
Okay.
In your own time.
In your own time.
Are you going to do this?

Steve Give me a chance.

Peter I'm really starting to freak out, can you please shoot me?
You have done this before, haven't you?

Steve More or less.

Peter What do you mean, 'more or less'?
   I thought you were a hit man.

Steve I never said that.

Peter You kind of implied it.

Steve When?

Peter When you agreed to kill me for money?

Steve I normally just beat people up.

Peter Look, if you don't want to do it, give me my money back and I'll find someone who can.

Steve No.

Peter Well, get on with it then.
   Will the gun make a noise?

Steve It's got a thing on it.

Peter A *thing*?

Steve (*raises gun*) Count of three. Three . . . Two . . .

Peter Wait.

   Pause.

On one or after one?

Steve What?

Peter Are you going to do three two *one*. Or three two one *go*.

Steve On one.

Peter On one.

Steve All right.
   Three . . . Two . . .

   Silence.

Peter Please.

Steve You'll have to get someone else, I'm sorry.

Peter Why?

Steve It's not right.

Peter I'm asking you. It's a compassionate gesture. I'm insured for this. My wife will get the money.

Steve Why do you want her to have money?

Peter I want to provide.

Steve Can't you just talk to her?

Peter Look at me. It's practically euthanasia, and that's legal in Switzerland. We'll set our watches forward an hour pretend it's Zurich.
    Pretend I'm someone you hate. Who do you hate? Come, there must be someone.

Steve My dad.

Peter Your dad! Pretend I'm him. Shoot me. Pretend I'm your dad.

Steve He's already dead.

Peter It's pretend.

Steve I think you should get someone else to do this.

Peter I don't know anyone else who kills people.

Steve I'll find someone.

Peter We have to do it now.

Steve Why?

Peter I'm shitting myself. Please. As a man.

Steve Some people should never be born. Used to call us cunts. Used to call everyone that. That was his word.

Knocked her about. Even when she was pregnant with Sis. Mum drank herself to death 'cause of him.

Have this dream, I'm playing with my boy. He's got his back to me. Sun's out. Grass, flowers, laughter. He turns around, my boy. He's got dad's face.

I've got to kill him. My own boy, 'cause if I don't he'll turn into Dad, and I can't allow that. But if I kill him, then I turn into Dad. Do you see?

What do I do?

Tell me what to do.

Peter Look at me.
Look at me.
Son.
Steve.
That's it.
Look at me.

Steve raises the gun.

Steve I kill you, then I'll be you.

Peter It's all right.

Steve No.

He lowers the gun.

Peter Look at me.

Steve No.

Peter Look at me, you cunt!

Steve raises the gun.

Pull the trigger. And it's over. I'm gone.

Steve But then I'm you.

Peter No.
Come on.
You can do it.

75

You can do it.
You can do it you can do it you can do it.

Steve Cunt!

Steve turns the gun on himself and pulls the trigger.
Click. He pulls the trigger again. Click.
  He tries a third time. He can't.

Peter What happened?

Steve I've never fired a gun before.

Peter Did you load it?

Steve I think so. (*He checks.*) Yes.

Peter Is that supposed to be like that?

Steve I don't know.

Peter My whole life. It's true. In a flash.

Steve Any good?

Peter Not really.
  Don't think you're getting paid.

Steve Do you want to try again?

Peter takes the gun.

Peter I don't understand.

Steve Would you mind not waving it at me?

Peter It doesn't work. Look.

SEVENTEEN

Hard, discordant, black metal, and blurred, grainy
pornographic film, like a flood.
  The film burns and melts.

We hear Ralf's laughter, distorted.
Perhaps it is the laughter of the city.
The scene has the quality of a dream.

EIGHTEEN

Soley's Bar.
   Steve, Soley. Steve's foot is in a cast. He walks with a
crutch.

Soley What happened to your foot?

Steve Health and safety.

Soley What kind?

Steve Some bloke shot me in the foot.

Soley Do you have a union?

Steve Did you hear me? I said he's not coming back.

Soley I know.

Steve How?

Soley He told me.

Steve You saw him?
   When did you see him?

Soley I told him I would go with him. I told him I would
do whatever he wanted me to do. But I told him I could
never love him.

Steve So he just went.

Soley Yes.

Steve I gave him the money.

Soley Why did you do that?

Steve So he'd go.

Soley He didn't want the money.

Steve So why did he take it?

Soley If someone gave you money, would you take it?

Steve When did you talk to him?

Soley A few days ago.

Steve Cheeky bastard.
He won't be coming back. I know the type.

Soley Yes, you do, don't you?

Steve What do you mean?

Soley Where did you get the money?

Steve Compensation.

Soley For what?

Steve The health and safety.
I'm not lying.
It's not what you think.

Soley How do you know what I think?

Steve You're looking at me different.
The person who gave it to me made me promise not to say.
I made a promise.
I didn't kill anyone.
That guy in the bar. The one who walks around the world. He gave it to me.

Soley He just gave it to you?

Steve Yes.

Soley No one just gives money like that away.

Steve Ask him.

Soley Oh yeah, the guy who walks across the world and spends all his time getting jerked off in my bar, he's reliable.

Steve You don't trust me.

Soley You don't get things for free. Everything costs something.
  I need to go away.

Steve I'll come with you. (*Pause.*) Why not?

Soley I'm tired of being fought over. I'm not a prize.

Steve I love you.
  I need you.

Soley We need each other.

Steve So stay.
  Thought you liked me.

Soley You're a good man.

Steve Then why won't you be with me?

Soley I'm a cat and you're a dog.

Steve Stop saying that. It's just something you say. I'm not really a dog. You're not really a cat. You said we need each other.

Soley Need is not good.
  I will never be who I am with you around.

Steve You don't mean that. (*Beat.*) Where will you go?

Soley (*shrugs*) Back home, maybe.

Steve Back to him.

Soley Somewhere nobody knows me.

Steve I can't live without you.

Soley Yes, you can. For Sarah.

Steve She doesn't need me.

Soley I was saying that to be nice.
I'll pay you the money back.

Steve Okay.

Soley Actually, I don't think I can. I was just trying to be English.

Steve I'll name you my price.

Soley I need to be free.

Steve A song. Sing me a song. One of your songs. To remember you by.

NINETEEN

Soley's bar.
  John, Peter. Cups of tea or coffee.

Peter Sat next to each other in after-school science club. Used to do experiments. Right nerdy little couple. Had these intense arguments about methodology. It was our way of flirting.

John She always used to drink cider when we argued. I didn't know if it meant anything. Some small rebellion or . . . Drove me round the bend.

Peter We used to cycle up the rec (the recreation centre) up to a fishing pond. Pretend we were fish. They always seemed so happy. Obviously they used to get caught and it can't be nice having a hook in your mouth, but at least the get thrown back. Pick up a bottle of cider from the local offie. First time we had sex (and it was the first time) we got drunk on cider. Used to do that a lot. Till Glenn, her stepdad, changed job and she moved away. You ever see them, her mum and Glenn?

John Came down for the funeral.

Peter Grumpy old sod, isn't he?

John Why did you want to walk to every country on earth? Your profile –

Peter Oh yeah.

John Is it a private joke?

Peter No. Think I just wanted to be somewhere else. I just couldn't make up my mind where.

John I became her friend. Had to get in touch with Facebook, 'cause she couldn't accept me, obviously. Things she wrote. The clothes business. Things she could've done, things I didn't support her in. I told her to buck up. Vampires. Who's God?

Peter What?

John God.

Peter Oh. Mr Armstrong. Ran the science club. Big white beard.

John I don't think I did her justice.

Peter You mustn't say that.

John Did your wife really leave you for your dad, or did you make that up?

Peter No, that's true.

John Do you see them?

Peter Seen Rachel. Not Dad. Tried to win her back.

John How'd it go?

Peter Brilliant. Can't you tell?

John How do you carry on? What do you do?

Peter Day after I found them I went in to work. I worked with my dad. Wasn't in that day. Had our own architecture firm. I was working on a hotel leisure complex. I sat down at my desk and sketched out a building shaped like a big cock and balls. It was rather good. One was a solarium and sauna, the other was a restaurant. It was very detailed. Foliage round the front as well, shrubs and things, you know.

John Right.

Peter And on top of the building there was a rooftop pool inside a sort of dome structure with a retractable roof. Thing I was most proud of was, you know, there was the sauna and solarium bit and the restaurant bit?

John Yeah.

Peter (*gestures*) The sauna and solarium was slightly bigger. Most satisfying day's work I ever did.
  You know the worst thing?
  I think they're right for each other.
  Actually that's the second worst thing.

  A Waitress enters, played by the same actress as Nicola. She collects the empty cups.

Worst thing is, I still miss him. Can you believe that?
  (Could I get some water please?)

Waitress Sure.

John Should go and see him.

Peter No.

John Why not?

Peter I just. No.

The Waitress brings over some water.
    Peter opens a small case, removes a tablet, swallows it with water. John watches the Waitress.

John Sometimes I see her.
    Nic. I know it's not her, but I have to look twice. And when I look back . . .

The Waitress exits.

She's gone.

Peter What I said. The last time. I'm so sorry. I don't think that's what Nic really thought about you at all. You could see she . . .

John At the wake, everyone was coming past and, you know, 'So sorry to hear,' and 'Our thoughts are with you,' 'Such a tragedy' . . . and my nephew Michael – who's six – was with my sister and his dad, and he said, 'She was hit by a car, wasn't she?' And I said, yes. And he said, 'What kind of car was it?' And I said, a Peugeot 206. And he said, 'Oh.' He looked really disappointed. My sister and Gerry looked mortified, but I started laughing. Then I went down the bottom of the garden and cried. And smoked a spliff. Which Glenn thought was disrespectful, but by then I didn't care. There will always be a place for honesty, always. Not cruel honesty. But . . . straightforwardness.

Peter Shit.

John What?

Peter Are you Buddha in disguise?

John laughs, mimes a fat Buddha. Peter laughs.

John The night she died, I fucked someone. That's why I didn't answer my phone. I'd never done it before. I thought Nic didn't understand me.

Peter I don't know what to say.

John (*a flash of anger*) You don't have to say anything, you just have to listen.

I felt so grown up. Like I'd finally become a mature adult, you know, broken the shackles of conventional morality. I thought I had all these unique feelings. That I was special. But actually it just made me like everyone else. 'Cause everyone feels special when they're cheating on someone, don't they?

I dream a lot now, never used to. Used to sleep like a baby. Last night I dreamt I was in the lobby of the hotel with this other woman. And she asks me to come up to her room. And my phone goes. And I know if I take the call Nic won't die. But I turn off the phone. Then I wake up. I've had that dream a few times. And I never take the call.

Peter (*pause*) I read the paper while I was waiting.

John Any good?

Peter We're all in debt, no one's got a pension, we can't afford houses, we all hate our job. The icecaps are melting, wars, bombs, floods, famine – you know, real problems, big enough for Madonna to get involved. What is there to do? Apart from sit and watch *Big Brother*. Wasting your time is the only rational response to the world. We're fucked. Oil, climate change, it's gone, it's done. We've missed it. Haven't we?

There's got to be more than this? Otherwise there's no point to anything. Love's not just a form of behaviour management.

John No.

Peter It's real.

John Yes.

Peter It has to be.

John Things matter. They shouldn't, but they do. Go and see your dad. Go and see him. Tell him that you love him. Tell him that you miss him. Tell him he's a cunt and he's ruined your life, just tell him something. Will you do that?

Peter We're all fucked up really, aren't we?

TWENTY

Sarah's new flat.
   Sarah, Steve. Steve holds a plant pot in a sunbeam in the middle of the room. He is still on a crutch with his foot in a cast. There is a watering can.

Steve Here?

Sarah Yes.

Steve You sure?

Sarah Definitely.

Steve I think it needs to be nearer the window, sweetheart.

Sarah You said it needs to be in the light.

Steve The light's going to move, darling.

Sarah Well, I'll move the pot wherever the sun is.

Steve What, you're going to stand there all day?

Sarah Yes.

Steve This is silly, I'll move it by the window.

   John enters.

John Knock knock. Hello, Sarah. Hello. See you're still moving in. I'm in between visits so I can't stop. I brought you this. I remember you said you liked it, so I – flatwarming.

John hands Sarah the carved wooden cat.

Sarah Thank you. That's nice – isn't that nice, Steve?

Steve Yeah, it is.

John looks at Steve's cast.

I shot myself in the foot.

John I'll pop by.

Sarah Yes. For a cup of tea!

John leaves.

Clumsy.
For you.

Steve No, it's yours, sweetheart.

Sarah Flatwarming present.

Steve You're supposed to give the present to the person moving in, not the other way round.

Sarah Well, we're being different.

Steve Leave it on the side.

On the same stage, Peter enters Soley's Bar in Iceland. He wears lycra.

Sarah You ever hear from her?

Steve Got a postcard, actually. From Iceland. Didn't say anything. Just a picture. Of a fjord.

Soley enters the bar. She sees Peter and brings him a vodka.

She told me fjords made her feel calm.

Steve hands Sarah his phone. She changes the ringtone and passes it back.

Sarah Will you go looking for her?

Steve shakes his head.

Why not?

Steve 'Cause she's a cat and I'm a dog.
What do you do if you get lost in a forest in Iceland?

Sarah Don't know. Buy a map?

Steve Stand up. (*Beat.*) Where d'you want this?

Sarah I've told you, in the sunbeam. That's where
sunflowers go.

Steve I'm putting it by the window.

Sarah I'll only move it when you're gone.

*Steve leaves the plant pot in the sunbeam. He opens a
packet of seeds, passes them to Sarah.*

Steve Plant it deep, make sure you water it.

*Sarah pushes the seeds into the pot and waters it. Steve
and Sarah stare at the nascent plant.*
Soley sings the most beautiful song in the world.
*It is beautiful, not because she has the best voice, but
because it is true.*
*The sun has moved round a little. Steve moves the
pot back into the light. The cat is now in the sunbeam
too.*

Sarah Perfect.

Acknowledgements

In 2003, in an Old Vic rehearsal room, five actors from Liminal Theatre presented nascent versions of characters. I asked them questions, took notes and proposed ideas for scenes. Over the next few years we persevered with this collaboration in the form of several workshops, discussions, improvisations, arguments, and an invaluable week at the NT Studio.

Songs of Grace and Redemption would not be the play it is without the talent, enthusiasm, and creative endeavour of its many conspirators, who include: Ian Midlane, Asta Sighvats, Melissa Woodbridge, Solveig Gundmundsdottir, Sally Leonard, Charlotte Randle, Paul Ready, the ever-patient Sarah Sansom, and in particular, Robert Reina and James Hurn, who have given so much to the characters of Peter and John.

I also wish to thank: Liminal's artistic director, Janette Smith, for her unwavering commitment to the text, her generosity of spirit and mind, and her invaluable midwifery; Reynir Eggertsson and Maria Dalberg for the Icelandic; Simon Trussler, for not throttling me; the Peggy Ramsay Foundation, for putting food on the table; Lisa Foster, Dinah Wood, Chris Campbell, Ruth Little, Richard Bean, Simon Stephens, and all others who have kept my chin up and my glass full; Tim and Paul at 503, for their taste.

It was done, like all folly, with the best intentions

JD, October 2007